THE PASSENGER'S PALACE

100 YEARS OF CUNARD BUILDING LIVERPOOL

THE PASSENGER'S PALACE

100 YEARS OF CUNARD BUILDING LIVERPOOL

Written by: Michael Gallagher and Tony Storey
Production Editor and Design: Harri Aston
Design: Chris Collins
Published by Trinity Mirror Media
Managing Director: Steve Hanrahan
Commercial Director: Will Beedles
Executive Editor: Paul Dove
Executive Art Editor: Rick Cooke
Marketing and Communications Manager: Claire Brown

The authors and publishers are grateful to the following individuals for their time and help in providing material for this book: Jim Ashcroft, Val Ashcroft, Joan Bernard, Pam Birch, Carole Black, Muriel Bradbury, Pamela Brown, Marjorie Brundrit, Pat Dempsey, John Flamson, Joe Garnett, Jenny Higham, Rhona Letley, Joan Maxwell, Marie O'Neill, Malcolm Perry, Hilary Taylor, Sian Wilks.

Images used in The Passenger's Palace have been supplied by: Cruise Media Services, Cunard, Cunard3queens.com, Ray Farley, Gareth Jones, Mills Media, Mirrorpix, PA Images, Paul Ward.

First Edition
Published in Great Britain in 2016.
Published and produced by: Trinity Mirror Media,
PO Box 48, Old Hall Street, Liverpool L69 3EB.

ISBN: 9781910335420
Printed and bound by Buxton Press

Contents

To my Dad. For always being there and just for getting through it.
Michael Gallagher

The Pilots of the Fleet Air Arm.
Tony Storey

Foreword

I have witnessed some extraordinary events in Liverpool during my close association with the city which now spans almost four decades.

One which evokes the most vivid memories, and which had such a profound impact on all who saw it, was the majestic gathering of Cunard Line's Three Queens on the Mersey in May 2015 in their spectacular salute to Liverpool.

Together with my family, I watched the huge ships perform their remarkable river dance from the windows of Cunard Building, the striking edifice at the centre of Liverpool's UNESCO World Heritage Site waterfront.

It was a day and an event which positioned Liverpool on a world platform, a position the city must strive to maintain in our fiercely competitive global markets.

Darker days have, of course, dawned over Liverpool but I have always been struck by the resilience of the city and its people, not to mention the powerful spirit of enterprise and innovation which is so evident.

Those attributes were, I am sure, much in evidence when Samuel Cunard started his passenger shipping service from Liverpool to North America in 1840. The rapid growth of his business necessitated the creation of a new world Headquarters. The fact that the great Building – The Passenger's Palace – was conceived, designed and constructed during the Great War is further testament to the vision and determination of both those who commissioned its construction and those who toiled so tirelessly to build it 100 years ago.

As well as its important function for Cunard Line, Cunard Building has been home to many other businesses and organisations. Among these was Government Office North West which occupied the wonderful ground floor spaces to oversee so much of the regeneration and development of the city as we see it today. Now, it is entirely fitting that the city's own administration is based here as Liverpool continues to reach out to the rest of the world for new opportunities for growth.

The Passenger's Palace provides a fascinating record of this great Building, its functions and the memories of many of those who worked within its walls.

Lord Heseltine
June 2016

The Pier Head: Hub of an Empire

Few waterfronts in the world are as identifiable or admired as that of the Pier Head in Liverpool and for a century the Three Graces – the Royal Liver Building, Cunard Building and Port of Liverpool Building – have stood as visible symbols of Liverpool's international prestige and proud emblems of its commercial prowess.

These three architectural masterpieces are a sight beloved by all Merseysiders, countless passengers, seamen and tourists over the years. It truly is a waterfront on a par with New York, Hong Kong and Sydney.

All three of the Graces occupy the site of the former George's Dock, which was the third dock built in Liverpool and completed in 1767.

By 1898, George's Dock was essentially redundant and closed as it was too small and shallow for the commercial ships of the late 19th century.

After the extension of both Water Street and Brunswick Street to the river frontage, George's Dock was destined to transform from a workaday dock to one of the finest waterfronts in the world. Most

Liverpool's iconic Three Graces, as seen in the 1980s, with Cunard Building standing in between the Royal Liver Building, left, and Port of Liverpool Building

Liverpool's landing stages
during Victorian times

Liverpool from the Mersey in 1837 and, below, the last days of George's Dock

of the site was owned by the Mersey Docks and Harbour Board, while a smaller part was still held by the Corporation of the City of Liverpool.

The Board and the Corporation had differing priorities, and the former was not inclined to forgo any commercial advantage for the benefit of the latter.

In January 1896 the two bodies began discussions, with the Corporation seeking to persuade the Board to accept its offer to buy the site and reserve a portion of it for new Board offices.

Two years later, a deal was agreed whereby the Corporation paid £277,399 for the site, from which the Board reserved about 13,500 square yards for its own building. The Board pressed ahead with its new Headquarters and announced a competition, restricted to local architects.

A neo-baroque design was approved, with a central dome added just before the start of construction in March 1903, and the Mersey Docks and Harbour Board Offices – more commonly known as the Port of Liverpool Building – was opened in the summer of 1907.

The Corporation had been confident of finding tenants for the two remaining plots suitable for large-scale buildings but no such

prospective tenants came forward. It was decided to offer the freehold of the sites for sale but there were no bidders at an auction of the sites in 1905.

The following year, the Royal Liver Friendly Society made an approach offering £70,000 for one of the plots – considerably less than the £95,000 the Corporation had hoped for.

The Mersey Docks and Harbour Board expressed consternation at the height of the Royal Liver Society's proposed new Headquarters but after much debate the Corporation approved the plans and the Royal Liver Building opened its doors in 1911.

But what was to take the central site – what was to become the centrepiece of one of the most famous trio of buildings in the world?

This centre site would prove the most difficult to develop, with various plans and ideas submitted during the first decade of the 20th century.

Initially, some city councillors thought it would be the ideal site for the new public baths while others favoured a new tramway office for Liverpool's expanding tram system. To appease both groups in 1902, ▶

The Three Graces act as screens for the light show as part of Cunard's 175th anniversary celebrations in May 2015

a competition for a combined baths and tramway offices was organised and 17 designs were received.

The competition had stated that any new structure should be in keeping with the Port of Liverpool Building which was Edwardian baroque in style and, in October 1903, a design similar to that building, with a tower rather than a dome, was unveiled.

An agreement could not be reached on the exact design so all submitted proposals were rejected and the whole matter was referred back to the Baths and Tramways Committees to prepare their own schemes.

After the Pier Head Baths closed in October 1906 the empty central site was earmarked for a combined Baths and Customs House but this scheme collapsed when funding for the latter was refused by the Government.

Three years later, the Baths Committee abandoned any hopes of developing the central block and acquired adjacent land for the new public baths.

At the same time, the Corporation gave building contractor William Cubitt & Co a five-year option to purchase the central site and in 1912, under further pressure from the Chamber of Commerce, Cubitt commissioned a commercial scheme incorporating a Customs House.

The building combined elements of the Port of Liverpool Building, crowned by both a dome and a tower, but again the Government refused to get involved. Finally, just as Cubitt's option was to expire, a new buyer was found: Cunard.

Secrets of the Palace

England's annual Heritage Open Days provide members of the public with a rare opportunity to see places normally beyond their reach.

The joint venture, managed across the country by the National Trust, funded by Historic England and the People's Postcode Lottery and delivered locally by landlords, owners, tenants and an army of volunteers, allows people rare access to hidden architectural gems.

With its wealth of fine buildings, the city of Liverpool has long been a major contributor to the national Open Day programme – and places for tours of Cunard Building are booked up within hours of being made available.

Apart from these few days in September, the Building is not generally open to the public – a far cry from its heyday as the Passenger's Palace.

Interest and intrigue in the famous Grace spreads far and wide though, and hopeful visitors regularly arrive on the Ground Floor hoping to see and share its secrets.

Whenever possible, Building Manager Joe Garnett and his team try to accommodate casual visitors.

At the very least, these wide-eyed arrivals in reception will take away a printed history sheet prepared by Joe's team, and – access permitting – a glimpse inside the former Ground Floor booking and embarkation halls. With their necks craned, they will gaze up from reception at the magnificent central staircase lined with etched renders of Cunard's famous travel posters.

"Every day we have visitors and tourists wanting to tour the Building," says Joe. "We explain it is a working building and cannot allow people to wander around. We do, if possible, show them the Ground Floor and give them an historical fact sheet on the Building. We tried to use different languages for the fact sheet, which became quite challenging."

Joe was appointed Building Manager in May 2002.

"I was very, very proud to be appointed at Cunard. I felt I had reached the pinnacle of my career as a Building Manager," says quietly spoken, impeccably dressed Joe. "I was amazed at the size of the building, and tended to get lost from time to time."

He displays a pride and passion for working in the Building as well as a professional expertise in ensuring it operates and is maintained to the highest standards expected by its multiple tenants – tasks which present their own challenges.

"Cunard Building is very challenging mainly because of its Grade II listed rating. Maintaining the high standards of the Building and keeping occupiers happy is very testing. There was always a sense of achievement when completing major tasks. One of the biggest being when the exterior cleaning took place in 2010."

Since 2007, the successful development of Liverpool's cruise operation, attracting ever-increasing numbers of ships and their guests to the waterfront, has led to a steady increase in casual visitors arriving at the Building. Many are keen to blend their sea-going

Building Manager
Joe Garnett on the
Ground Floor

experience with the history and heritage associated with the former Headquarters of the most famous name in passenger shipping.

"The main impact on the Building is the visitors off the cruise ships wanting tours.

"The Building was purpose built for shipping and with the name of Cunard the link is fairly obvious. More so when any of the Cunard Queens call at Liverpool," says Joe.

Externally, with its position between two stunning neighbours, some visitors sometimes feel Cunard Building is overshadowed. It is a perception soon lost on those lucky enough to see inside.

"The Three Graces complement each other," says Joe. "The Port of

Liverpool is pleasing on the eye, intricate and imposing. The Liver Building gets all the publicity because of the Liver Birds but Cunard has all the history and heritage associated with a world-renowned company."

Film and television location managers have a particular fondness for the Building as well as an appreciation of the efforts of the city's Film Office (based on the Fourth Floor) to facilitate their often demanding visits.

Cunard Building has become a popular spot for filming in recent years, with film-makers able to take advantage of its grandeur, and recent TV filming has included ITV's *Foyle's War* and Sky 1's *The*

Cunard Building has played a part in the filming of several films and television dramas, including Florence Foster Jenkins, starring Hugh Grant; Foyle's War and Peaky Blinders

Five. For several months in 2015, filming for *Fantastic Beasts and Where to Find Them*, the highly anticipated adaptation of J.K. Rowling's Harry Potter prequel, took place in the large space on the Strand side of the Ground Floor.

"We have welcomed a number of screen stars," Joe reveals. As he reels of their names it is clear some made a more positive impression on the Building Manager than others.

"Geraldine James, Michael Kitchen, Cilla, Sheridan Smith, Steve Mangan, Meryl Streep, Hugh Grant, Steve Redgrave and Simon O'Brien have all been here in recent years. Managing the needs of productions like *Foyle's War*, together with keeping the building running smoothly with minimum disruption to those working here, is always a challenge," admits Joe.

Despite welcoming famous names inside the Building, Joe remains adamant that events outside during 2015 to mark the 175th anniversary of Cunard's first sailing from Liverpool to North America is the memory he will recall most clearly in years to come.

"The best was seeing the Three Queens sailing up the river and then dancing into position. The worst was the long hours we put in over that weekend, but it was an amazing event and one we were all proud to be part of."

So much of Cunard Line's own history is embedded in the fabric of the Building it is not difficult to stand in silent rooms and imagine what momentous decision were taken – decisions influencing the Company, the city and the country.

"When I stand in the rooms, the history seems to pour out of the walls," says Joe. "Like myself, the teams I have worked with adore the building and care for it as if it was theirs."

Today, the Passenger's Palace remains resplendent – thanks in no small part to Joe Garnett.

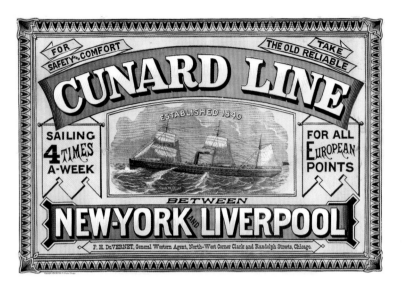

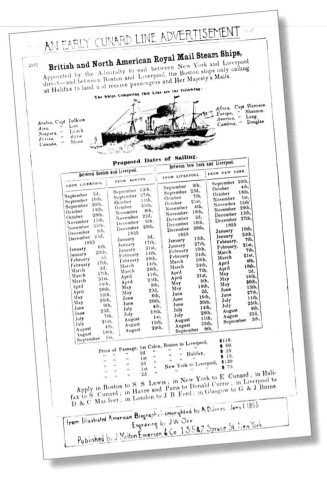

Home is Where the Heart is

Liverpool is the birthplace of Cunard and, from its inception in 1839 until 1967, the Company had its Headquarters in the city. In those 128 years three offices were home to British and North American Royal Mail Steam Packet Company – thankfully known from the outset as Cunard.

The first office was established at 14 Water Street and this is where the fast growing business remained until August 1857 when Cunard simply outgrew those premises and moved to 8 Water Street.

The 14 Water Street site would be demolished to make way for Oriel Chambers, which was one of the world's first buildings featuring a metal framed glass curtain wall when it was completed in 1864, and it is today home to barristers' chambers.

The new office at 8 Water Street, on the corner with Rumford Street, was soon to become the hub of an enormous business, concerned not just with shipping across the Atlantic to the United States and Canada, but also with routes to ports in the Mediterranean and Middle East.

But, of course, a shipping company is not just the ships – there is a vast backroom operation making travel arrangements for passengers in many countries, ordering supplies from food to coal, coordinating repairs and servicing, dealing with Customs and the administrative requirements of the countries served, planning and executing the construction of new ships and so on and so on.

Following a further half century of persistent, if erratic, growth into ▶

The view from Seacombe
promenade in July 1913

8 Water Street as Cunard's Head Office and, right, today. Below, Oriel Chambers today

one of the notable companies of the world, Cunard was ready by 1911 to embark on the creation of a magnificent landmark building having once again outgrown its existing office. The site of 8 Water Street is today occupied by a concrete office block.

Cunard's desired new Head Office location was not far – the Drury Buildings just across Water Street. It had a large basement, frontages on Water Street and Drury Lane, and could be accessed at the back from Back Goree.

By April 1912 plans were advanced for Cunard to acquire the Drury Buildings and the adjacent Brazilian Buildings (with its frontages on Drury Lane and Brunswick Street). A total of £170,000 had been allocated for the purchase of the two buildings, the subsequent conversion and compensation to the existing tenants who would have to move out.

On 2 May 1912, Cunard made an option money payment of £500 on the Drury Buildings to secure the site for 21 days while it proceeded with negotiations with the existing tenants.

This process was more difficult than anticipated, with some of the tenants reluctant to move. This, together with the fact that Cunard had never built from scratch its own Liverpool base or Head Office, put the George's Dock site within Cunard's sight.

Here the Company could build a palace meeting its own exacting standards – while a refurbished Drury Buildings would make a fine Head Office it was still originally built in the 1850s so Cunard would be moving into a 'new' 60-year old building. The message Cunard would send out by building on such a prestigious waterfront site could not be underestimated.

Today the India Buildings, constructed between 1924 and 1932, stands where the Drury Buildings and Brazilian Buildings were located.

Despite having to share the George's Dock site – one third of the land being allocated to the new Customs Office – Cunard acquired the eastern portion from Cubitts for £60,000.

Cubitts would construct the new Building at their own expense with Cunard guaranteeing to rent the property for 30 years before taking over ownership.

The Corporation would only approve the new Cunard and Customs buildings if their designs complemented each other. Fortunately, the Government would scrap plans for the new Customs Building so Cunard would have the whole site to create its new magnificent palace that it had now agreed to rent for 75 years after its completion.

A report to Cunard Directors stated: "The premises at 8, Water Street, Liverpool, being no longer adequate for the requirements of the Company's business, the vacant portion of the site of the George's Dock, Liverpool, has been acquired, and a large Office Building will be erected thereon.

"Arrangements have been made for borrowing on favourable terms the amount which it is estimated this building will cost, secured by a mortgage on the property."

By June 1912 it had been agreed that Cubitts would erect a

"respectable" building on the George's Dock site for Cunard "not to cost more than £200,000" and that Cunard would buy the freehold and mortgage.

Cunard committed to build on the George's Dock site on 1 July and on Saturday 21 December 1912 completed the purchase of the site with a transfer of £68,000 to Cubitts. A balance of £36,716 would be paid at a later date.

The future Passenger's Palace was on its way.

An Architectural Masterpiece

After deciding to construct a new landmark office on the Pier Head, Cunard had to tackle the issue of its external design. The two buildings on either side were both massive and ornate so should the central edifice be even more massive and more ornate? In tune with Sir Samuel Cunard's plain and simple philosophy, the Board opted for understated although the Building would deliver some awe-inducing statistics.

In October 1912 Cunard appointed Liverpool-based architects William Edward Willink and Philip Coldwell Thicknesse to design their new Building. The Company had earlier worked on Franconia (1910) and Laconia (1911) and its assistant architects Harold Dod and Watson Cabre were given the Cunard Building project to work on.

Cunard also employed the services of London-based Charles Mewes and Arthur Davis to work alongside the Liverpool architects. Mewes and Davis had submitted their own design schemes to Cunard for the new Building several months before the appointment of Willink and Thicknesse.

Inspiration for the interior would be taken from Cunard's floating palaces Lusitania and Mauretania, which had entered service in 1907, and Aquitania which was then under construction and whose interiors ▶

"Over the years stories have surfaced claiming that Cunard Building was originally to be twice as high"

were the responsibility of Mewes and Davis and had impressed the Cunard Board. Davis had also earlier been responsible for the Ritz Hotel in London, Piccadilly and the RAC Club on Pall Mall.

As is always the case with great projects, several schemes for the new Building would be drawn and developed and these offered different treatments of the Ground Floor openings, different main entrances and more subtle variations of proportion and finish.

Originally, the Greek style was favoured but the height of the Building itself did not favour this style.

Over the years stories have surfaced claiming that Cunard Building

was originally to be twice as high, making the top of the Building the same level as the Liver Birds on top of the building next door. The fact Cunard Building had a flat roof and could easily have received a slightly narrower building on top in a phase two of construction adds weight to those who believe there was to be a phase two – and the fact New York's Cunard Building reached 23 storeys hinted that its Liverpool counterpart could have reached further upwards.

In February 1913 it was decided the new Building would take its influence from the Italian Renaissance and the grand palaces of Italy. This style had been argued for by Arthur Davis and it was relatively

simple, devoid of flounces and based on the Farnese Palace in Rome which had been completed somewhere about the middle of the 16th century for Cardinal Allesandro Farnese, later Pope Paul III.

But the Cunard Building was to be much, much bigger. Big enough, in fact, for 250,000 people to stand inside - and over 1,000 people would work in the Building over its 11 floors. Despite the strong Italian influence, the architects did retain a Greek style for the details around the Building itself.

The Palazzo Farnese is an imposing Italian Palace dating from the 16th century and is one of the most important High Renaissance

The final design for
Cunard Building

The Palazzo Farnese and, below, the initial Cunard Building design

palaces in Rome today while currently serving as the French Embassy in Italy.

Construction began in 1515 for the Farnese family and when Alessandro Farnese became Pope Paul III in 1534 the size of the palace was increased significantly. Michelangelo was employed to redesign the Third Floor with its deep cornice and he revised the courtyard as well.

The Palazzo's design has been copied for several buildings outside Italy, including the Detroit Athletic Club in Detroit, Michigan; Château Grimaldi near Aix-en-Provence, France; the National Building Museum in Washington, D.C., USA; the Chief Secretary's Building in Sydney, Australia and the Royal Palace, Stockholm. In England, Charles Barry's great admiration for the building led him to use it as the model for London's Reform Club and, of course, Cunard for its new Headquarters on Liverpool's Pier Head.

By February 1914, plans and a model of the proposed Building was presented to Cunard's Board, with formal approval being given in April.

Of the Three Graces, Cunard Building occupies the largest ground area, but since Water Street and Brunswick Street are not parallel, the plan is a trapezium with nine bays on the east and west sides, and seventeen bays on the north and south sides.

However, as it was constructed after the Port of Liverpool Building and Liver Building, on either side of it, space limitations meant that the east (landward) side was actually built 30 feet (nine metres) wider than the west. The central bays on each side provide the main entrance points into the Building. Each entrance consists of a large panelled oak door, adorned by a pair of fluted columns and with a coffered ceiling.

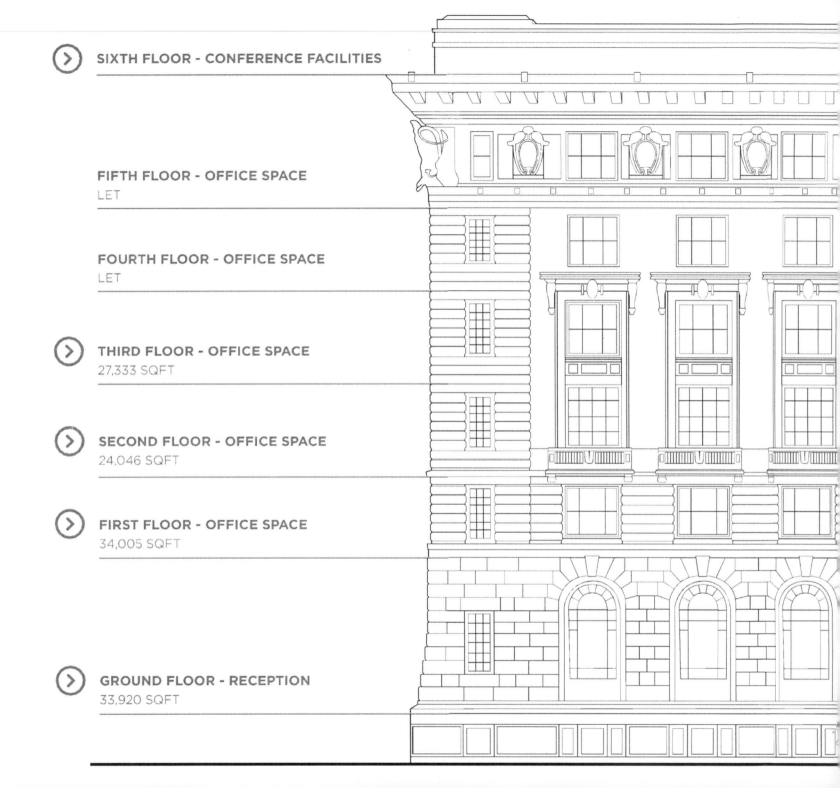

SIXTH FLOOR - CONFERENCE FACILITIES

FIFTH FLOOR - OFFICE SPACE
LET

FOURTH FLOOR - OFFICE SPACE
LET

THIRD FLOOR - OFFICE SPACE
27,333 SQFT

SECOND FLOOR - OFFICE SPACE
24,046 SQFT

FIRST FLOOR - OFFICE SPACE
34,005 SQFT

GROUND FLOOR - RECEPTION
33,920 SQFT

An illustration used in a
promotional booklet for
Cunard Building in 2008

STREET LEVEL

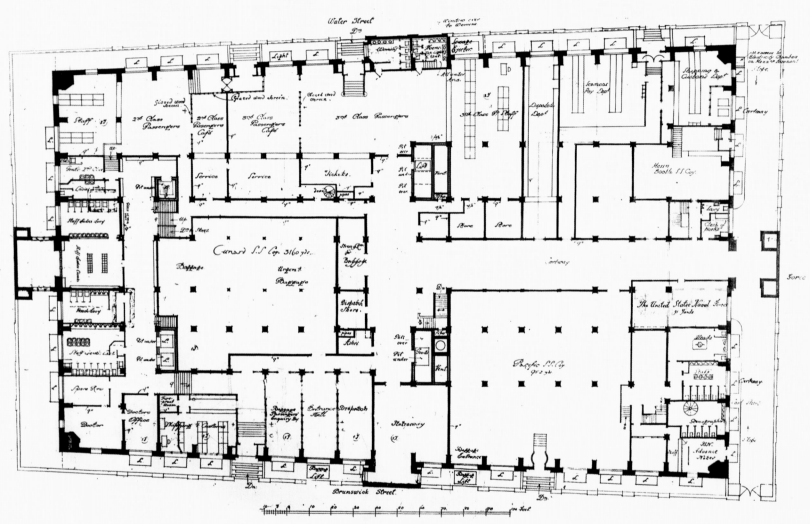

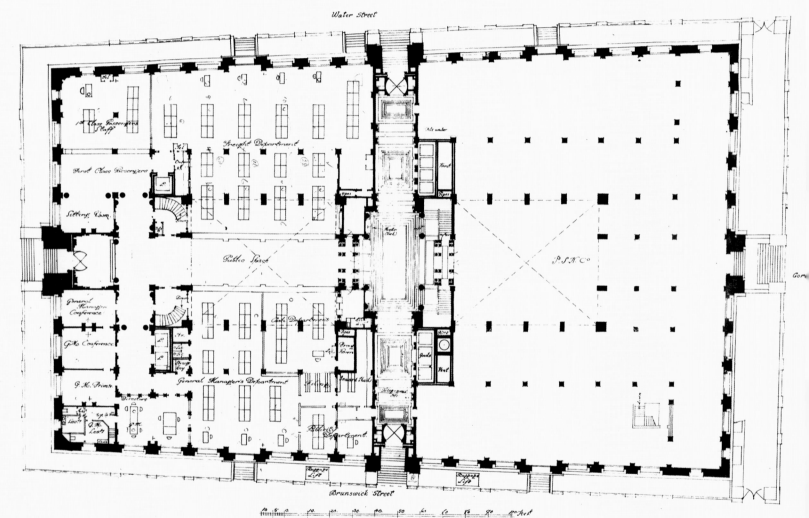

Water Street

Pierhead

Gore

Brunswick Street

1st Class Passengers Staff

First Class Passengers

Sitting Room

General Managers Conference

G.M. Conference

G. M. Private

Directors

Lav'y

Freight Department

Cash Department

General Manager's Department

Publicity Department

Public Space

P.S.N.Co

Baggage Lift

Baggage Lift

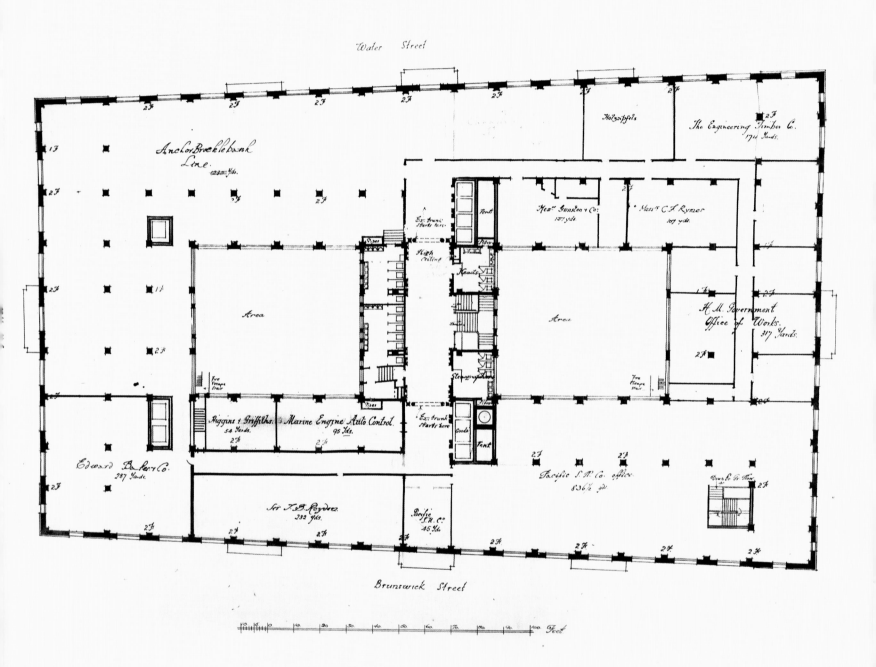

Water Street

Anchor Brocklebank
Line
1230 Yds.

Holzapfels

The Engineering Timber Co.
1711 Yards.

Mesrs Gunston & Co.
157 yds.

Messrs C. I. Rymer
107 yds.

Area

High
ceiling

Heads

Area

H. M. Government
Office of Works.
317 Yards.

Stenographers

Fire
Escape
Stair

Fire
Escape
Stair

Edward Bates & Co.
287 Yards.

Higgins & Griffiths.
54 Yards.

Marine Engine Auto Control.
95 Yds.

Goods

Pacific S.N. Co. office
536½ yd.

Sir T. B. Royden.
232 Yds.

Pacific
S.N. Co.
45 Yds.

Brunswick Street

0 10 20 30 40 50 60 70 80 90 100 Feet

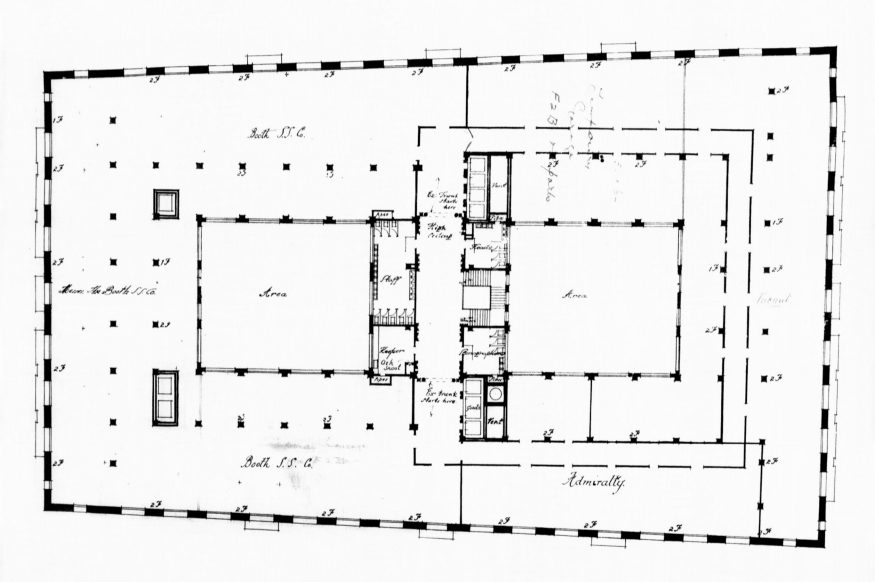

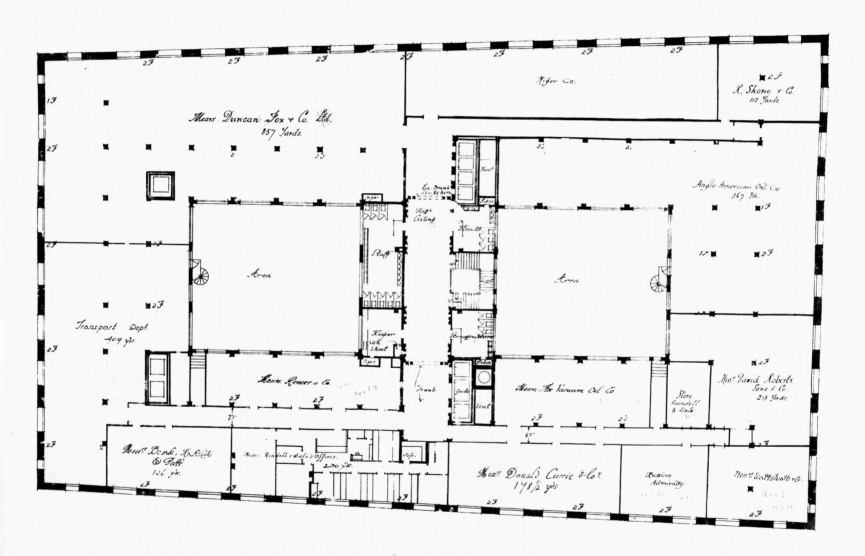

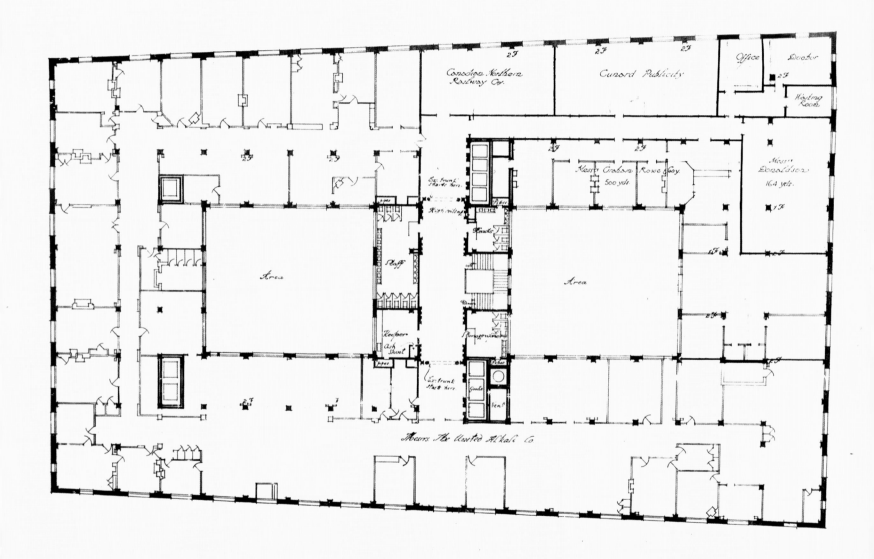

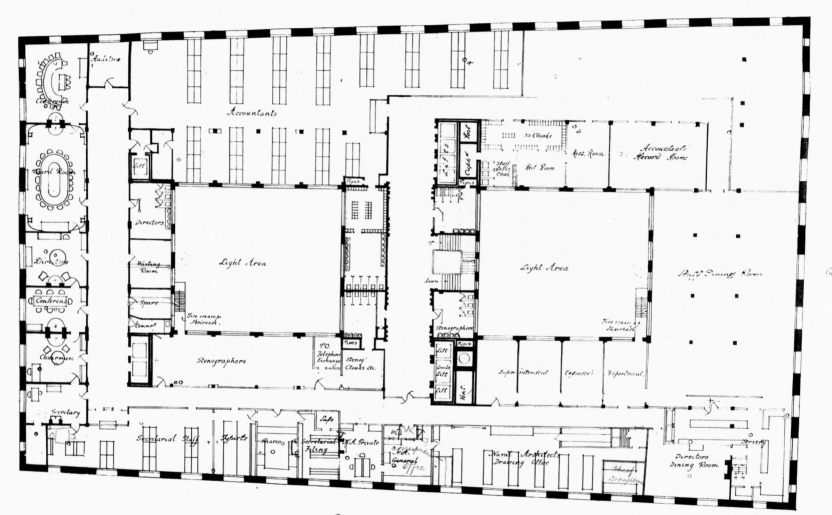

Water Street

Accountants

Auditors

Committee

Board Room

Directors

Directors

Conference

Chairman

Directors

Waiting Room

Spare

Commee

Fire escape Staircase.

Light Area

Stenographers

Secretary

Secretarial Staff + Experts

Shares

Secretarial Filing

P.O. Telephone Exchange

Stenog Cloaks etc.

Times

Safe

V.A. Private

Correspondence General Office

Naval Architects Drawing Office

Chief Draughtsman

35 Cloaks

Retd. Room

Accountants Record Room

Lifts

Hoist

Cafe

Staff Ladies Cloak

Rest Room

down

Stenographers

Light Area

Staff Dining Room

Lift

Goods Lift

Lift

Vent

Superintendent Engineer's Department.

Fire escape Staircase.

Servery

Directors Dining Room

Brunswick Street.

10 20 30 40 50 60 70 80 90 100 Feet.

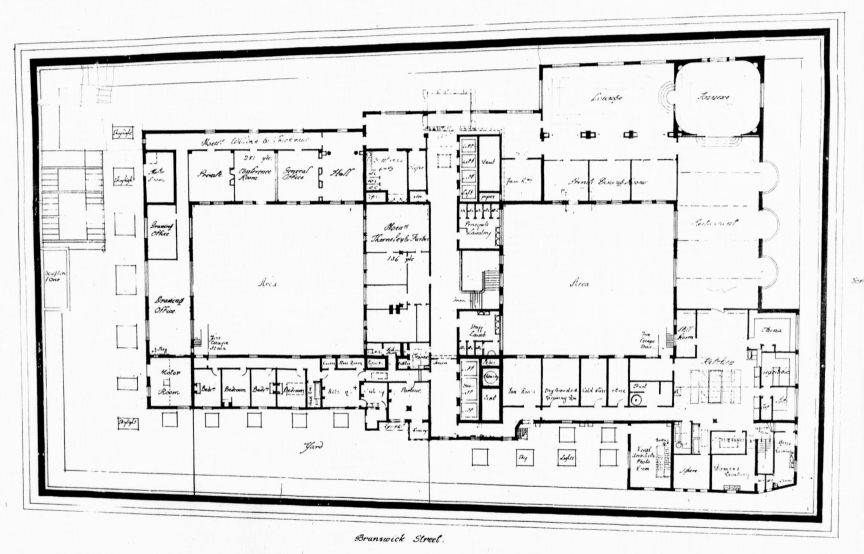

Water Street

Brunswick Street.

Scale of Feet

Building Manager Joe Garnett standing next to the original dock wall

Cunard Building has a length from the front façade on the Pier Head to the city façade of 330 feet, the width of the former being 170 feet and the latter being 200 feet. The height from the Basement is 125 feet, and from the foundations in the bed of the old George's Dock 170 feet. The areas of floors totalled 50,130 square yards (nearly 11 acres).

The Building stands six storeys tall and features two basements, a raised ground floor and five upper floors, with further accommodation provided in the roof. Due to its construction on the site of the former George's Dock, part of the original dock wall is visible today in the eastern boundary of the first basement level and evidence of water seepage clearly seen.

An indication of the Building's huge size can be found in the fact the projection of the beautifully proportioned cornice is seven feet nine inches along the sides, and no less than 12 feet at the corners, though when seen from the roadway nothing like this amount of overhang is suggested!

Portland stone on the exterior of the Building was selected for its durability. Sir Christopher Wren selected the stone for St Paul's Cathedral, maintaining that it had no equal for withstanding the smoke of London and the fact that it could withstand all types of weather, and the Pier Head has always been exposed to extreme atmospheric conditions.

The Building itself would stand on a sloping rusticated base built of rough bug stones from the Roach quarries of Portland. The large plain wall surfaces were broken only by the rusticated angles and the

windows on the First Floor. The Fourth Floor windows were kept absolutely square and devoid of decoration to emphasise the greater elaboration of the parts above and below them. Above is a highly-decorated frieze with a heavy projecting cornice surmounted by a plain wall.

The projecting doorways, though rough in general outline, were treated with great refinement in the porticoes, and the heavy arched windows on the Ground Floor further tend to enhance the finished simplicity of the other parts of the Building. The carving was not only decorative but would become of increasing historical importance as

the Building aged as the subject selected drew attention to the period of war during which the construction took place.

The façades of the Building were adorned with great features of the Italian Renaissance. The true line of the Building begins above a Greek Wave Course which surrounds the exterior of the edifice above the Ground Floor at a height of 30 feet from the road level. Below this course the walls are battered giving the appearance of massive strength and solidity.

The masonry below the wave course is heavily rusticated with each piece being distinguished by a broad surrounding channel, while the chiselling of the protuberant stone faces is rough which increased the impression of rugged strength and forcefulness.

This rustication is continued up the piers or masses of walling at the four angles to the frieze, which encircles the Building just below the cornice. Elsewhere, the stonework of the façades is smooth and polished.

On the front (western) façade, which owing to the shape of the site is the smallest of the four containing walls, there are 54 openings, all of which, except the main doorway, are windows. Those in the rusticated piers at the ends of the façade are plain, oblong, light

43

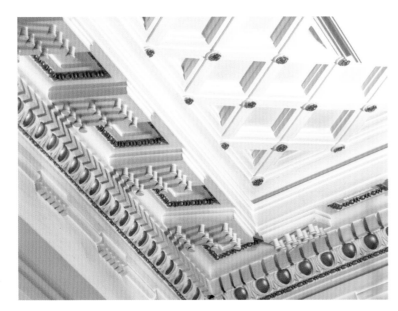

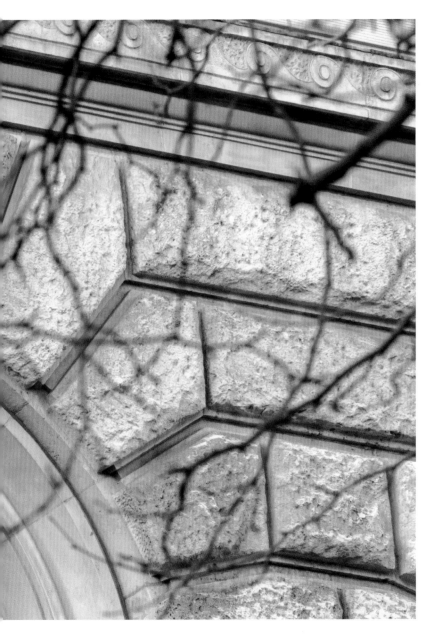

openings, with a height twice their breadth. The advanced doorway is surmounted by a balcony guarded by lions displaying the Shield of England. On either side of the doorway are three large windows, each 25 feet in height, crowned with semi-circular arches, the keystones of which, like that of the arch over the doorway, are carved in bold relief, with emblematical heads and nautical devices, depicting such objects as storm, calm, peace and war.

Above these arches runs the Greek Wave Course. The series of windows immediately above are flat headed, simple, light opening devoid of all ornament, but with the glazed portion subdivided by plain mullions into one large and two narrower lights. The windows of the next two storeys are arranged in vertical pairs, the lower of each having a balcony, and the upper surmounted by a cornice supported by corbels.

The jambs are carried from the balcony to the window heads, upon each of which is carved the Coat of Arms of the then principal passenger ports in the United Kingdom: Liverpool, London, Bristol, Southampton, Plymouth, Falmouth, Hull, Newcastle, Portsmouth, Glasgow, Leith, Aberdeen, Dundee and Queenstown (Ireland not being an independent country at that time).

On the north and south sides of the Building over the Third Floor windows were placed Signs of the Zodiac while over the doorways and on the projecting base are to be found Storm and Neptune, Peace and War, Britannia and typical faces of the Dominions – an Indian American, an Aborigine and an Afro Caribbean.

Above the line of cornices is a row of windows, corresponding to those immediately above the rusticated and battered portion of the Building. These are separated from those under the grand cornice by an architrave with a key ornament cut on it relieved by medallions. On the voids between the uppermost line of windows are bold carvings, displaying the shields of the Allies, while at each end of

45

the line, and connecting the western with the northern and southern façades is a great eagle supporting the shield of the Cunard Company – each weighing 43 tons.

The Shields of the Allies, Britain, France, Russia, Italy, Japan, Belgium, Serbia and Montenegro, acknowledged the troubled times of the Great War in which the Building was conceived. The United States is missing as the construction was completed before America entered the war.

Possibly the great doorways set in the centre of the east, north and south facades appear even more impressive than that on the Pier Head front, a possible result of the greater length of these sides of the building. Each doorway is approached up a flight of stone stairs and flanked by a pair of bronze lamps with fluted columns, claw feet and acanthus leaf shields set on huge stone plinths.

The general disposition of the Building was absolutely simple, four entrance doorways in the centre of the two sides (on Water Street and Brunswick Street) give access to a broad corridor from which all the offices were approached, the upper ones by means of six lifts and one goods lift.

Some 50,000 cubic feet of finest Italian and Greek marble, from Attica, Carrara and Arni Alto was lavished on the massive public rooms, corridors and stairways all adorned with marble columns and floors. Coal was also stored in the Basement with a small railway track providing a link to the boiler room which was used to heat the Building.

Cunard Building was lit by electricity and, in all, there was a 80,000 feet run of conduits which equalled 15 miles. There were about two miles of steel-armoured main cable and if the component copper wired in the same were measured separately, they would equal 50 miles. Light cable equalled 40 miles and if all the component wires were measured separately they would equal 200 miles.

Bells, telephones and clock wires equalled 21 miles and the component wires of the same separately would run to about 74 miles.

Lavatory accommodation was provided on several floors and a separate wardrobe was provided for each employee so that offices were not cluttered with unnecessary apparel.

The original plans included shops, a tea room, a rifle range on the sixth floor and a Turkish Bath in the Basement – none of which were built.

According to Cunard publicity at the time of the building's opening: "The architects are, therefore, to be congratulated upon having produced a building which so satisfactorily fulfils the underlying motive of the ablest exponents of the art of the Italian Renaissance, namely, to erect in stone a picture which would appeal rather by its homogeneous symmetry and general charm than by the beauty and intricacy of its individual parts. In fact, they have achieved more than this, for they have adapted the beauty of the Italian Palace to the strenuous conditions of the business life of a bustling British seaport."

Building the Third Grace

Work would progress on design and construction relatively rapidly after Cunard purchased the site in December 1912, with occupation of the Building scheduled for the end of 1915. The foundations and basements started that month and the whole development was expected to cost £280,400 (February 1913 estimate).

Construction of Cunard Building would be entrusted to Holland, Hannen & Cubitts, established in 1883 and responsible for many important structures. They include, in London alone, the Prudential Insurance Building in High Holborn, the Cenotaph, London County Hall, South Africa House, the Senate Building of the University of London and the Royal Festival Hall. It also built the Roxburgh Dam in New Zealand and the Trawsfynydd nuclear power station in North Wales.

When the engineers came to prepare for the site of Cunard Building they had to prevent any water flowing in at high spring tides, so the old dock walls were reinforced with 700,000 cubic feet of concrete, weighing 45,000 tons, that was reinforced with 2,000 steel bars which would measure 1,000 miles if they were all lined up. The

The groundwork being prepared for the construction of Cunard Building

How the site looked
on 28 July 1913

28.7.13.SB.3

Images of the Royal Liver Building being constructed between 1908 and 1911

floor of the dock became the floor of the lower level of the Building's two basements.

At the Brunswick Street side of the site a reinforced concrete wall was built 300 feet in length, which shut out the tidal water rising and falling in the existing arches under Brunswick Street, while along the river front a mass concrete wall, eight feet thick, was constructed before the work of preparing the foundations could proceed.

The foundation of mass concrete piers was built on the rock bed which underlay the surface clay at the Pier Head end of the site. The foundation piers ranged from four square feet to eight feet nine inches square, the latter running up to the underside of the mezzanine floor and forming the bases for the reinforced concrete columns which bear the weight of the superstructure.

Around February 1914, work began on the Building's superstructure. The frame was constructed from reinforced concrete, built using the Kahn system by the Trussed Steel Concrete Company, which was then clad with about 150,00 cubic feet of Portland stone, weighing about 10,700 tons.

In addition, 650 cubic feet of granite, weighing about 55 tons, was used on the exterior. The largest stone in one piece weighed eight tons

and special lifting devices had to be employed for the manipulation of that piece and other large blocks.

As work progressed, changes were made to the design including the addition of a Sixth Floor and, in July 1914, the estimated cost of the Building had increased to £348,829 thanks also to "other alterations" and extra costs of work on its shell. By completion the Chairman, Alfred Booth, was able to report that savings of £20,199 had been achieved resulting in a revised cost of £328,630.

The eruption of the First World War on 28 July 1914 would change the world and everyday life beyond comprehension and it is incredible to think that Cunard Building's construction continued as the conflict raged in Europe.

At this time the Cunard Empire included repair shops, laundries, engine works, and furnishing departments as well as the army of clerks and administrators – almost all of them based in and around Liverpool.

So, on the outbreak of war, as well as continuing to repair and service the Company's own ships, the repair shops and engine works were also given over to military use, servicing and maintaining naval craft; the laundries, hitherto dealing with all the linen taken from

A view of Liverpool's waterfront before Cunard Building was built

ships now also gave themselves over to dealing with laundry from military hospitals.

In what was an enormous undertaking, not least for a business with no experience of building planes, the Cunard aeroplane factory was established at Aintree in 1917 and within a year 5,000 people were turning out 100 planes a month.

One of Cunard's vast warehouses in Bootle was given over to the manufacture of shells and became the Cunard National Shell Factory. More than 1,000 people, 900 of them women, worked 24 hours a day, seven days a week in three shifts, from October 1915 until November 1918 when it closed down within a week of the Armistice being signed.

All told, the factory produced 410,302 shells. All of this going on as

Cunard Building rose seemingly in defiance on the Pier Head!

In April 1915, Cunard announced it hoped to start occupying their its Head Office by the end of the year, as the upper storeys of the Building were nearing completion.

But perhaps it was inevitable that such an ambitious building programme would be affected by the war as a few months later Cunard announced that: "The erection of the Company's new Office Building at the Pier Head, Liverpool, has been greatly delayed by the inevitable shortage of labour.

"It is now proposed to move the Company's business to the new premises during the month of June [1916]."

While a six-month delay is a blow to any development, it is still a great feat to have been able to restrict the hold-up to just six months. ■

Construction work progressing
in September 1914

Full Steam Ahead

The first staff began to move into Cunard Building – now clearly the Headquarters of a company that mattered – over the weekend of 10 and 11 June 1916, with various departments gradually relocating from Water Street. There was still a great deal of work to be completed, and hoardings would remain in place around the Pier Head frontage for several more months, but Cunard had arrived and for the next 51 years the Building was the centre of the shipping line's world.

Cunard Building was perfect in every way, not just for the reassurance its air of permanence and solidity given to nervous passengers, and not just from the efficiency inherent in having all the staff on one site, but because the directors could look out of their Fifth Floor Board Room window and see all the cohorts of their empire – the ships – coming and going from the Mersey.

On Monday 12 June 1916, Cunard Building was opened without formality or fuss. The Liverpool Daily Post said the Building was "the very last word in commercial architecture" and "a palace on the riverbank which sets a standard for the envy and emulation of all cities in the Kingdom".

The newspaper predicted that Cunard Building would do Cunard

Cunard Building pictured in August 1916 with hoardings around the Pier Head frontage remaining just a few weeks after its opening

Cunard Building in 1920

"A palace on the riverbank which sets a standard for the envy and emulation of all cities in the Kingdom"

Line 100 years and that it had the "finest range of architectural interior" in Liverpool.

The company said: "Cunard Building at once conveys the idea of stability and durability, while the great spaciousness and comfort within make it the finest shipping office in the world. Completed during troublous times, it is striking evidence of the immense development of the Company which we are so proud to serve."

The Building was always going to offer more space than even a shipping mammoth like Cunard ever required so it was always the intention to rent space to other tenants. The initial yearly rents

collected by Cunard would total £14,594, of which the Cunard Steam Ship Co would pay £11,231 for its use of space in the Basement, Mezzanine Basement, Lower Ground Floor, half of the magnificent Ground Floor, and the Fourth, Fifth and Sixth Floors.

Cunard Building was home to several other important shipping companies from 1916, including Cunard's Anchor-Brocklebank (First Floor), Booth Steamship Company (Second Floor) and the Pacific Steam Navigation Company which took space in the Mezzanine Basement, the Lower Ground Floor, the First Floor and one half (The Strand side) of the magnificent Ground Floor space.

From the opening of the Building until the 1960s, the list of tenants reflected Liverpool's mercantile credentials and included Ed Bates & Sons (merchants), Rundell & Dale (average adjusters), Canadian Northern Railway Co, Banks Ratcliffe & Potts (timber merchants), the Liverpool Corporation, ICI, Lever Brothers, Spillers, Sun Life and The Admiralty together with a host of coal merchants, iron merchants, steel merchants, timber merchants, cane merchants, steamship brokers and millers. The Building's architects, Willink and Thicknesse, also had offices here in the early 1920s.

In April 1917, Cunard Chairman Sir Alfred Booth reported at the Annual General Meeting: "We moved into our new premises in this Building last June. This is a bald statement of great event. As a matter of mere capital expenditure the Cunard Building may be a small affair compared with the Aquitania, but it will stand as monument of the Company's progress and of this great period long after the Aquitania has been forgotten. You have seen the Building for yourselves, inside

and out, and I am sure you will agree with me that it is worthy of the Cunard Company, worthy of Liverpool, and worthy of the British Mercantile Marine."

In January 1918 the first 'Cunard Magazine', a monthly publication issued to give all Cunard staff updates on "the doings of colleagues on active service" as well as inform those staff fighting in Europe on the "doings at home which, though very tame in comparison...", was launched. In the Foreword, Sir Alfred wrote: "The coming of the war strengthened and deepened the sense of comradeship, and the Cunard Building has provided us with means of expression in many directions that were not possible before."

'Cunard Magazine' discussed a wide range of subjects including socks: "Who would have thought four years ago that the now magical word 'socks' could bring such a gleam of happiness into the tired eyes of a 'line soldier'...."

The Cunard Comrades Fund was established at the start of hostilities. When the call for volunteers was made in August 1914 a large number of Cunard staff immediately offered themselves. In view of this remarkable response, a meeting of the Heads of Departments

The first edition of Cunard's staff magazine and, right, Army recruits being inspected by Birkenhead MP Alfred Bigland outside Liverpool's St George's Hall during the First World War

Queues for the luggage boats can be seen in this view of the Pier Head from 1919

was called for on 4 September for the purpose of creating a fund for the interests of the men while they were away on service, assisting their dependents financially or with advice as required, extending support to the men themselves in time of difficulty and generally helping in forwarding comforts which might be called for by the sacrifices they had so willingly made.

Cunard was very proactive during and immediately after the war when it came to staff welfare. Entertainment was arranged in the Staff Dining Room for wounded soldiers of the various hospitals in Liverpool and many river trips, picnics and days out were arranged to lift the spirits. Over the festive period, the Cunard Board welcomed and served soldiers Christmas lunch with Father Christmas in

Aquitania, seen here in 1914

The Mauretania, pictured above, operated from Southampton from 1919. Right, Cunard Building in New York

attendance. As the men left the Building there were each presented with a souvenir box containing a pipe, tobacco, cigarettes, matches and a packet of interior view postcards of Aquitania. Each box bore the inscription: "With the Best Wishes of the Cunard Steam Ship Co., Ltd."

After the war, those injured or maimed were retained by the Company to perform various tasks in the Building.

The end of war brought about a significant change in Cunard operations when the Company decided to relocate its express Atlantic service to Southampton. From 1919, both Mauretania and Aquitania would operate from the southern port – much to the relief of Captains, who found the vagaries and vicious tides of the Mersey a constant trial, but simultaneously to the dismay of Liverpudlians.

However, White Star's express service had been operating from Southampton since 1907 and it still had its Head Office on the Pier Head, so perhaps Liverpool had nothing to fear from this move.

The intermediate Atlantic service to New York and services to Canada would continue to sail from Liverpool but the fact was the Company's most prestigious and biggest ships were now based elsewhere and not where the business itself was headquartered.

On 2 May 1921, the 23-storey Cunard Building in New York opened and both buildings were compared to bookends on the Atlantic.

Throughout the mid-1920s the Chairman Sir Percy Bates developed his vision of two ships maintaining the weekly express Atlantic service instead of three. They would be the "smallest and slowest" ships to do the job but they would emerge as the fastest (Queen Mary) and largest (Queen Elizabeth) liners in the world.

The launch of the second Mauretania

And while neither Queen would ever visit the Mersey they did have Liverpool emblazoned on their sterns as port of registry, and the most successful double act in Atlantic history will always be linked with Cunard Building.

Financial difficulties and the desire to complete the Queens resulted, after Government intervention, in Cunard and its rival White Star merging.

On 1 January 1934, the first day of the new Cunard White Star Company, staff from White Star had to cross the Strand and proceed to Cunard Building where the White Star buttons on their uniforms were cut off. The newly-named Cunard White Star Line would be based in Cunard Building.

White Star was then housed in Albion House, on the corner of James Street across from the Pier Head. After many years being

The second Mauretania setting sail on her maiden voyage to New York in 1939

vacant, the building was converted into a Titanic-themed hotel in 2014 known as 30 James Street

Sir Percy would have been able to keep a close eye on the construction of the second Mauretania, which was built across the river and launched into the Mersey on 28 July 1938 by his wife. It is fair to assume Cunard Building would have provided a grandstand view that day with its windows filled with staff all keen to get a view of the new ship taking to the water. It would have been the first time most of them would have seen the launch of a company ship as the majority of Cunarders had been built on the Clyde in Scotland.

During the Second World War, the sub-basement level of Cunard Building was utilised as an air raid shelter for workers in the Building and also for those from adjacent premises. The basement levels also served as the central Air Raid Precautions headquarters or command centre for all Liverpool air raid wardens.

Additional reinforced steel joists were fitted to further strengthen

the Basement in case of a direct hit, and the American Consulate became a tenant in the Building.

Liverpool was the most heavily-bombed area of the country outside London due to the city having, along with Birkenhead, the largest port on the west coast and being of incalculable importance to the British war effort.

Thankfully, the Three Graces escaped being heavily hit and remained largely unscathed but there are stories of incendiaries being cleared from the roof of Cunard Building.

In 1950 when Aquitania, the Ship Beautiful, was finally retired after 36 years of loyal service to her owners, the ensign flown on her final voyage was presented to Cunard Building and was placed on display in the main foyer. Aquitania had been the only liner to serve in both world wars.

From January 1963 the cleaning of all offices and common parts of Cunard Building was taken over by Office Cleaning Services Ltd with a weekly charge of £135.15.0. or £6,955 per annum. The cost to Cunard of employing its own cleaners had been £12,266 per annum.

The £5,311 per annum savings had been gained by the introduction of machines for polishing and scrubbing.

In February 1963, Cunard Properties Limited was formed and all Company properties, including Cunard Building, were transferred from The Cunard Steam-Ship Co. Ltd to the new organisation.

On 12 July 1966, English Heritage awarded Cunard Building Grade II listed status – defining it as "a particularly important building of more than special interest"'– in a move that initially saw the Three Graces brought together under a Pier Head listing. This would be amended 20 years later when in 1985 each building gained its own listing.

By the mid-1960s the focus of Cunard activity had shifted away from Liverpool. The city remained Cunard's administrative centre but everything administered was elsewhere. The biggest supplier of Company revenue was the USA and the home port for the Cunard fleet had been moving inexorably, and by now completely, to Southampton.

In 1957 aeroplanes carried more passengers across the Atlantic

The Three Graces were lucky to escape
serious damage during the Second World
War, although there were some near misses

This aerial view of a bomb-damaged Liverpool shows how the city looked at the end of the Second World War

than passenger liners and the number taking to the air rather than crossing by ship would increase yearly thereafter.

Cheap air travel by the early 1960s threatened Cunard's future and Cunard Chairman Sir Basil Smallpeice firmly believed the Company was "fighting for its life" and could only survive and flourish by "selling floating holidays instead of just a form of transport".

He was committed to his mission to "save Cunard, not only for its stockholders but even more for the sake of those who worked in it". His challenge was a daunting one as between 1961 and 1964 the Company's passenger business had lost £16 million, leaving it to live off its capital.

Within months of running Cunard, Sir Basil had put together a new management team, appointed consultants Urwick Orr and Partners to improve the organisation with a widespread brief and

asked The Economic Intelligence Unit to thoroughly review the cruise market.

The main "do or die" recommendations included a dramatic reduction in the size of the fleet, the relocation from the Cunard Buildings in Liverpool and New York, the closure of offices in London, Sydney, Paris, Le Havre and Dublin and a reduction of staff numbers.

Southampton rather than Liverpool would now be the UK base for Cunard operations so the Company began to search for a suitable new home as its premises at Maritime Chambers, used since 1919, were no longer adequate.

The former South Western Hotel was to become the new home of Cunard with the former hotel building being converted to provide office accommodation for the company. After 128 years Cunard

PRO PATRIA

The Grade II listed Cunard War Memorial is located on the west side of Cunard Building and stands in memory of the employees who were killed during the two world wars.

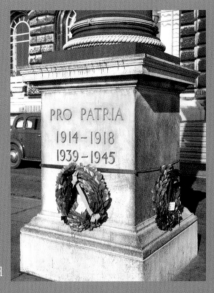

After the Great War, monuments and memorials would appear in village squares, towns and cities throughout the UK to honour the dead. Cunard approached Arthur Davis, who acted as consultant during the construction of Cunard Building itself, to design its memorial to the staff it had lost. In total, 13,000 Liverpudlians died during the war.

The erection commenced around 1920 and The Earl of Derby, Edward Stanley, unveiled the monument in October 1921 after it had been exhibited at the Royal Academy of Arts in London.

The monument consists of a large bronze statue that sits atop a Doric-style column, which is itself raised above the ground by a pedestal base. The statue was sculpted by Henry Alfred Pegram, whilst John Stubbs & Sons provided the stonework.

Davis designed the memorial to match Cunard Building's Greek features. The figure on top is of man, who is said to represent victory, standing above the prow of a Roman ship. Around him there are other naval references including ropes, anchors, and shells.

After the Second World War, the monument become dedicated to all Cunard employees who died in both conflicts. An

inscription on the side of the memorial reads "pro patria" (Latin for "for one's country"), and the years 1914 – 1918 and 1939 – 1945.

It is difficult to establish the exact number of Cunard personnel who died while serving their country. When the Lusitania sank, 401 crew perished alone. Many Cunard people received the D.S.O., D.S.C., M.C., M.M. etc and one was awarded the Victoria Cross.

On Wednesday 17 September 1952, two panels in memory of the sea-going officers and permanent shore staff of the Company who lost their lives through enemy action in the Second World War were unveiled by Frederick Bates, Cunard Chairman. The ceremony started with the lowering of Aquitania's ensign by the senior apprentice of the company, Cadet T Whitehead. After words from the Chairman and a short silence, both he and the General Manager laid wreaths at the foot of the panels and the ceremony closed with the raising of Aquitania's ensign. The plaques were relocated to the Church of Our Lady and St Nicholas, the Sailors Church, facing the Pier Head, in 1990.

Victims of the torpedo attack on the Lusitania, pictured right, are laid to rest in Ireland in 1915

"It's quite impossible directly to manage a factory from 250 miles away – I am sure none of you would attempt to do such a thing in your own business"

was effectively leaving home and the move was a huge blow to Liverpool, Liverpudlians and Cunard Building itself – which was still in excellent condition, worked well and did not look its age.

The Journal of Commerce and Shipping Telegraph asked: "What has made a great Liverpool-based enterprise like Cunard, with its long seafaring tradition, move to Southampton, away down in the "soft south"? What about the ships? What about the many Cunard men's families long established on Merseyside?"

The Journal did acknowledge that Cunard's ships still moved nearly a million tons of cargo in and out of Liverpool each year and the group still employed around 2,500 people in and around the city and spent some £6 million a year in the area on wages, harbour fees, stores and ships repairs, while Thos. & Jno. Brockelebank Ltd,

a key member of the Cunard group, was remaining in Liverpool.

Cunard Chairman Sir Basil Smallpeice responded: "It's quite impossible directly to manage a factory (which is what a base port is to us) from 250 miles away – I am sure none of you would attempt to do such a thing in your own business."

The existing Southampton staff of 200 would be increased with 120 moving from Liverpool and about 200 additional people being employed. Those who moved south were paid a disturbance allowance and a subsidy to reduce their mortgage interest to 3%, while those unwilling or not required received a redundancy payment.

Cunard was confident that as departments made the journey south the available space within Cunard Building would be let to outside tenants without difficulty. The first department to make the move was

Liverpool's New York service ended when Sylvania, pictured, sailed off for America in 1967

the Central Passenger Berthing and its ancillary sections in February 1966. The process continued and was complete by 1967.

Some passenger departments, and the Cunard-Brocklebank cargo division, would remain in Cunard Building but to all intents and purposes, Cunard had gone.

Sadly, Cunard had a rather cursory attitude to its archive and had intended to simply dispose of the vast collection of documents and ephemera it had built up over the 50 or so years it had been in the building. In fact, one future senior manager of Cunard would recall that on his first day at work in Cunard Building in the 1960s his first task was to destroy the photographs taken of the bodies washed ashore from Lusitania after she had been torpedoed in 1915.

With the move to Southampton ongoing, Francis Hyde, Professor of Economic History at the University of Liverpool, wanted to write the economic history of Cunard and asked if it would be possible to have access to the archive.

He was told to act quickly as it was in the process of being disposed. The professor and the university would remove a "mass of paper" from the Basement which today form the Cunard archive at the University of Liverpool.

Sylvania's departure for New York on 30 November 1967 would be the last sailing from Liverpool direct to New York but the final sailing from Liverpool would be made by Franconia on 30 January 1968 to Bermuda and then New York. Interestingly, Cunard announced that sailings had been "suspended" from Liverpool and not formally stopped!

THE PASSENGER'S PALACE

A Life Inside

Cunard Building would light-heartedly be referred to as "the Kremlin" by crews but there was always a sense of pride among those who worked inside it.

Cunard and the architects had ensured the future comfort of staff as the design had allowed for the "exceedingly liberal" amount of space per office and per worker, and the maximum amount of natural light.

The main entrance to the Cunard office was by the centre of the Pier Head elevation, while access could also be gained from the doorways on the north and south sides through the central hall. Entering by main entrance, visitors would pass up a short flight of steps and through a revolving door into the vestibule which formed part of one limb of a cross-shaped corridor, from which all apartments were approached.

Turning to the right, the General Manager's offices were reached as were two lifts, exclusively for the use of the Company, which gave access to the Lower Ground Floor and the Fifth Floor.

On the left of the cross-shaped corridor was the First Class Passengers' Department, including a sumptuous lounge.

Nearby was an automatic passenger lift that communicated with the floors upon which the Company's other offices were situated. The arm in the cross in front of the main entrance formed the approach

The General Office and, left, the departure lounge for First Class passengers as it appears today

to the General Public Office. The whole of the space was beautifully lined with marble, the columns being of Greek Pentelicon, the screens Italian statuary, while the floor of this cross corridor was paved in marble.

The Public Office, in which accommodation was provided for the General Manager's staff and Cash, Publicity, Freight and Saloon Passengers' Departments, reached from side to side of the Building and was in the centre lit by a glazed roof which came under one of the two great light areas. The whole space was dramatic with the roof being 30 feet from the floor.

The concrete pillars were all cased with marble from the Arni Alto Quarries with the same marble being used in all the screens of the

central office and in the counter fronts. When the Building opened, the matching space opposite was occupied by the Pacific Steam Navigation Company.

The wide public space of hall between counter and counter was, with the aim of ensuring silence, paved with linoleum, laid over sheets of cork, which gave a warm and resilient effect. The doorways at the east end of this main office space opened into the great central corridor which ran from Water Street to Brunswick Street and was handsomely paved with marble. From the entrance on the river façade could be found a striking vista through the Building from west to east.

In the Cunard General Office could be found the 'Captains' Room' where Cunard commanders, when ashore, could conduct their official correspondence and consult with the general staff on business matters on which they were mutually interested. Captains could exchange professional experiences and thus reciprocally assist each other in matters relating to navigation, winds, weather, ice movements, tides, currents and other subjects.

Below were the Mezzanine and Lower Ground Floors which by reason of the height of the Ground Floor above the pavement were well supplied with natural light. They were approached by three staircases and lifts. On the Mezzanine Floor were the offices of the Medical Superintendent, staff wardrobes and lavatories.

The Cunard Empire was now ruled from the Fifth Floor with a stately corridor with entrances to a fine suite of rooms facing the river, comprising Board Room, Chairman's rooms, Conference rooms, Directors' rooms, and a portion of the Secretarial Department.

In these series of rooms the decorative effect was concentrated on the Board Room which was a handsome, lofty and spacious apartment panelled in oak above which was a richly carved plaster cover with eight glazed elliptical windows, adding to the light from the two larger windows overlooking the river.

A private and hidden lift located near the Pier Head entrance could take six occupants from the Lower Ground or Ground Floor straight to the Board Room. For 50 years the key decisions that shaped Cunard's future were made here.

Some of the fireplaces, in the best Adams style, in the Cunard section of the Building, notably in the General Manager's and Directors' suites of rooms were, and today still are, exceedingly beautiful.

The rest of the Fifth Floor was taken up by large offices for the accountants, the secretarial staff, lady stenographers, dining rooms for the directors and staff and the pivotal naval architects' department, which would work on designs for three of the greatest Cunard ships ever: Queen Mary, Queen Elizabeth and QE2.

The 100-seat "high class" Britannia Restaurant and Lounge on the Sixth Floor, under Cunard management, covered about 400 square yards and was the highest restaurant in Liverpool. It had a barrel headed ceiling, three large bay windows and Adams-style furniture,

From top: The Board Room today, Staff Dining Room and Drawing Office for the naval architects

could be used by Building tenants or the general public, and was available for use for a Company meeting or evening lecture. Dinners were served a la carte, with catering and service the same as that found in First Class on Cunard ships.

On the roof, hidden from the street by the high parapet wall surmounting the cornice, were the keeper's house and the kitchens and larders that were necessary to supply the dining rooms, the Britannia Restaurant and a number of private luncheon rooms for the use of the firms occupying offices in the Building.

It was important to have adequate space for storing and handling baggage, and Cunard Building provided this. Passengers could arrive in advance and their luggage could be stored until sailing day. Inward passengers may have required their baggage to be forwarded, or they may have left it to await their return voyage. Inward baggage had

to be stored away from outward, and "wanted on voyage" from "not wanted". The baggage store occupied 570 square yards of floor space and was next to a large office for the baggage staff.

Several secure vaults, which in the past were used to store the most valuable passenger items, are still used today to hold historic documents, ephemera, drawings and blueprints relating to Cunard and the Building. Many original features of the Basement still exist, including the timber baggage racks which today house ship logs and other maritime documents.

Along the eastern façade of Cunard Building, running from ordinary road level to that of the Lower Ground Floor, were two sunken cartways which allowed baggage to be unobtrusively conveyed to the receiving entrance in the centre of the facade on the Lower Ground Floor for transmission to storage.

The Lady Staff Rest Room

One of the kitchens, where new recipes would be created for staff to try

General staff roles included battalions of clerks making bookings, ordering supplies, managing the to-ings and fro-ings of a large fleet, hydrographers mapping out the world's tides and an experimental chef whose job it was to try out new recipes on the staff before unleashing them on a doubtless more discerning clientele.

On the Fifth Floor was the Staff Dining Room which was a spacious area which included kitchens and service rooms fitted with the latest equipment. Juniors and those whose salary did not attain a certain standard dined free, with Cunard paying their contribution to the dining room accounts.

Dinners were served a la carte and teas were served to those whose work detained them after official hours. Adjoining the Dining Hall was a large smoke room for use by men.

Female staff had the use of the comfortably furnished Lady Staff Rest Room and their numbers were initially larger than normal in 1916 thanks to the large numbers of men fighting on the front.

Up until the 1950s staff will have probably taken the Liverpool

Overhead Railway, known affectionately as the "Dockers' Umbrella", which was the world's first elevated railway and operated long Liverpool Docks and had a stop on the Pier Head.

As a teenager growing up in Liverpool in the early 1960s, Carole Black used to accompany her mother on shopping trips to town, their Liverpool Corporation bus terminating at the Pier Head in front of the Cunard Building.

"We'd walk past the Cunard Building to go and get the bus home and I can remember looking down through the railings and seeing all the girls typing away in the stenographers' office and I said to Mum: 'I would love to work there.' And she said, 'Well, why you don't write in?' So I wrote a letter to Cunard and received a very nice reply inviting me for interview.

"Within a couple of weeks I was advised that I had been successful and was offered a position as a shorthand typist in the very room where, for nearly 12 months, I had been so desperate to work. What was really good about Cunard and working in the Building was that

Former Cunard employee Carole Black and, above, the Canning station for Liverpool's Overhead Railway

AWARDED BY
H.R.H The DUKE of EDINBURGH
To
Carole Ann Black
on attaining
THE GOLD STANDARD
of the
DUKE of EDINBURGH'S AWARD
11th May 1965

"For years after I left Cunard, whenever I walked past the Building, I would be filled with nostalgia"

they really got us involved in the business and what the business was about. We had to work in every single department. We dealt with correspondence from every area of the Company so got to know and understand an awful lot. After a while learning all that we were given a department to work for and I was given the Advertising and Sales Promotion Department.

"The Building was a very glamorous place to be. I was starting to get an interest in architecture and the Building is a great example of stunning design. There was a terrific buzz about the place and we were up and down to the various offices all the time to take shorthand notes."

As well as an exciting working environment, Cunard also offered staff the chance to travel at heavily discounted fares. "I went from Liverpool to New York in a First Class cabin on the Sylvania in 1966 and came back from Montreal for £20. I went with a friend, and it was a great adventure for two 21-year-olds from Liverpool," she says.

Carole's interest in architecture, allied to Cunard's supportive Personnel Department, led to her joining the Duke of Edinburgh Award Scheme and submitting an historical survey about the Building she worked in.

"I was given access to every part of the Building, places I never dreamt existed, even down where

CUNARD BUILDING

A million people lined the
banks of the Mersey to see
the QE2's spectacular maiden
visit to Liverpool in 1990

they were then still pumping water out, and I did a lot of research about the design and construction of the Building."

Carole's diligent efforts were recognised with both Silver and Gold Awards and after a spell working for Cunard in Southampton she returned to Liverpool and worked at the former Plessey telecommunications plant on Edge Lane.

"For years after I left Cunard, whenever I walked past the Building, I would be filled with nostalgia. It was a lovely place to work."

Marjorie Brundrit recalls her father's work at Cunard Building with palpable pride.

In 1964, at the age of 63, Robert Wood was due to retire from the Company he had served as a Naval Architect. Instead, he accepted a new role at Cunard Building as Chief Naval Architect. In postponing his retirement he embarked on a course which wrote a new chapter in maritime history – the creation of Queen Elizabeth 2, the greatest Cunarder of them all.

Although she was built on the Clyde and sailed from Southampton, everything that made QE2 the world-famous icon she became was decided in Cunard Building.

Joan Maxwell also has clear memories of the scale of the QE2 project inside the Building. She joined Cunard straight from school in January 1964.

"I worked as the Office Junior in the Company Secretary's Department on the Fifth Floor," she recalls. "Board meetings were held on the Fifth Floor too and all the Directors would sit around a long, polished table. This was where all the tenders for the QE2 were discussed and perused. All the tenders had to be packed away at night after the meetings and then safely locked away in a huge walk-in safe with a door so heavy I could hardly push it! Eventually, when all the tenders were let, the originals were all taken to one of the strong rooms in the Basement. Those rooms were a treasure trove of the history of the Company, completely fascinating."

"It was a fascinating place to work, full of hustle and bustle and I have many happy memories."

Despite being made redundant from her post in the Building, Joan Bernard has happy memories of her first job after leaving school.

"It was a fascinating place to work, full of hustle and bustle, and I have many happy memories"

"I started in the Publicity Department on the Sixth Floor in May 1960. My boss was a Mr Lobley, a lovely man who always arrived for work in a smart suit and, of course, a bowler hat. I was then transferred to the Shipping Department in the Basement working for new bosses who were also very good.

"The crew would come down and sign on in the Basement. Unfortunately, I was made redundant when the Shipping Department and the Sea Pay Department were combined – at that time girls were not allowed down on the docks, so a male junior from the Sea Pay Department was kept on. Overall though, working at Cunard Building was a very happy time for me, a time I will never forget."

Marie O'Neill joined the Company in 1954. "It was my first job and I worked in the Westbound Freight Department in the Basement of the Building," she explains. "It was a very happy office to work in and I only left after four years because the pay was so low!"

The complexities of running the global travel business from the Building are well remembered by Muriel Bradbury. "I was on the Tourist side, and used to do everything involved in arranging bookings and advising people on travel in the USA and Canada as well as answering most of the incoming correspondence using a Dictaphone which, at the time, was something very new indeed!

"I was given a red and gold 'Cunard Representative Pass' for boarding ships. With this I was able to have lunch on board when ships were in port."

Hilary Taylor's father was Joint General Manager of Cunard in

Here is Nerea Echave, a member of Cunard's typing pool, also pictured

the 1960s. "It was a great thrill for us to go down with our mother to meet him after work and run up the steps of the Cunard Building and ask to see Mr Taylor. His office was one of the big front rooms on the Ground Floor overlooking the Mersey. We also loved to look at the huge – to us – models of the ships displayed in the hall. We sometimes had Captains of the ships to visit us at home for a meal when they were ashore, and we often went to meet my father off the train from London at Lime Street, often with Sir John Brocklebank and Sir Basil Smallpeice who were travelling with him," she remembers.

"My parents were teetotal and when this was realised, one of the pre-Christmas thrills was to open the Fortnum and Mason hamper

The Accountants' Department

which would arrive for them instead of bottles of spirits. Imagine, in the late Fifties, having mock turtle soup and crystallised fruit!"

Rhona Letley worked in the Accounts Department on the Fifth Floor of the Building from 1957 to 1964.

"I was a very happy worker for Cunard. It was fun at work in the Building and a job I felt very lucky to have and I feel very proud when I think back," she says. "We used to have lots of laughs, and we were lucky to have a lovely restaurant on the Fifth Floor. After lunch we would go to a very nice rest room, some of us would take knitting and teach each other different stitches and the like. Now it would all be staring at mobile phones!

"There was a tennis team and I liked that. All the workers were

happy and good to work with. I was not the only happy worker either, and I was very sad when I had to leave – but very proud to say I was a worker in the famous Cunard Line."

At the age of 17, in July 1965, Pat Dempsey also joined the Accounts Department. "We had to start at 9am and sign in every morning. At 9am prompt a young girl world stride down the office and draw a red line under the last name to sign in! I was never late, so the system worked for me.

"The office was full of big shipping desks and you had to climb on stools to sit at them. I remember the lift operators wearing very smart uniforms and I believe a lot of them were, in the main ex-military men, some had been injured and stood down from regular duties. One ▶

Liverpool's Cavern Club, where many Cunard workers used to head during their lunch break

morning I walked into our office and the girls were standing on the big desks screaming. Modernisation was taking place and the desks were being moved and cockroaches were everywhere. My boss held one up and said it was one of God's beautiful little creatures and so on. It didn't wash with us girls!"

Cunard hosted staff Christmas parties in the Building each year. "They were something else," says Pat. "They took place in the canteen and everyone had too much to drink. There were always some red faces the following morning."

One shore-side perk of working for the most famous passenger shipping line in the world was to test menu dishes prepared in Cunard Building before they were served on board the liners.

"There was a big canteen serving tea, coffee and toast at morning break and full meals at lunchtimes. It also served full meals in the evening if you had to work late. I remember things like frog's legs being tried out. I have so many happy memories of my six years at Cunard."

Like so many Cunard employees in the Fifties and Sixties, Pam Birch was maintaining a family tradition when she started work at Headquarters at the age of 15.

"I went for an interview in 1959 to become a typist in the pool. The fact that my grandmother, grandfather and uncle all went to sea with Cunard meant that it was a case of keeping up the family tradition," she says. "After about a year a few of us were asked if we would like to join a new department – the Machine Room and Punch Room. It was the start of office computing and very exciting.

"We were there when the Merseybeat era really took off, so lunchtime was spent running up to the Cavern, listening and dancing to all the groups that later became household names. We then had to rush back, grabbing a cob for lunch.

Val Ashcroft, left, is pictured outside
Cunard Building with Marie Whelan

"It was such a happy office and a close-knit workforce. Each Thursday evening we did overtime and included in this was a dinner cooked by the trainee chefs before they went to the ships."

One of Val Ashcroft's recollections of working in the Building illustrates the scale of all operations taking place there – from designing ships to furnishing them.

"I worked in the Teleprinter Department and one day a couple presented themselves in our office saying I was wearing the exact colour they were looking for and would I go with them. It turned out they were photographers from the Naval Architects department and we trotted off to one of the ships outside, the Saxonia I think it was. They wanted to test the colour of my outfit against the décor of the dining room!"

The man who was to become Val's husband also worked in the Building where they met. Jim Ashcroft was based in the Accounts Department on the Fifth Floor between 1952 and 1956, leaving only to accept a place as a mature student at university.

"My job was preparing ticket receipts for each Westbound Tourist Class Voyage from Liverpool. We used to get requests from the American immigration service and the FBI about dates of birth and places and dates of embarkation of various passengers. The US Consul was based in the Building at the time. They were good times, very good times."

Even the vast roof of the Building was put to good use by Cunard engineers to test marine paint samples before they were approved for use on the fleet.

Engineer Malcolm Perry joined the company in 1961, working in the Design and New Construction Department.

"Two industrial chemists were employed and they would bring test panels of marine paint to locate on exposed area of the roof as a test to see how they weathered before being applied to the ships," he recalls. The high parapet surrounding the roof provides a wind break

Derek Jones, left, with Derek Spence from the Westbound Freight Department.
Pictured on the right is Valerie Barlow at the teleprinter

"We used to get requests from the American immigration service and the FBI about dates of birth and places and dates of embarkation of various passengers"

too and large "blue print" drawings from the Architects' Department would be laid out on the roof to dry.

"It was a great place to work and I remember on my first day there, having joined in a relatively junior position, being worried about being summoned to the General Manager's Office on the Ground Floor.

"I wondered what I could have done wrong so soon, but the summons was purely to be personally welcomed 'on board' in his palatial office looking out over the Mersey. This was something that inspired my loyalty from day one and typically reflected the prevailing company culture. I stayed with Cunard for 35 years."

Hundreds of Liverpudlian families would make weekly visits to Cunard Building to collect the wages of loved ones working at sea from the Lower Ground Floor Crew Department. There was a passageway outside the office with cubby holes where family members or crew themselves used to line up to wait for their pay which was handed through the cubby holes.

Cunard Building was a passenger terminal as well as Headquarters and within it were passenger related facilities for First / Saloon, Second and Third Class.

The premises at 8 Water Street had its Saloon Passengers' Department in plain old-fashioned offices that failed to give

Left and above, members of Cunard's football team. Right, a Spanish typist known only as Neria

passengers any idea of the grandeur and character they would find aboard ship. Now there was a booking hall, luggage storage space and a currency exchange and the public spaces were intended to evoke the same character and atmosphere as newly-embarked passengers would find on board.

On the Ground Floor was the enormous pillared ticket hall and lounge for First Class passengers with a view over the Mersey and Cunard publicity would stress: "The intending passenger visiting the Cunard Building must carry away a mental picture in which massive grandeur, chaste refinement, and a general pervading air of comfort have been artistically blended."

The walls, floors, counters and reinforced concrete pillars of the Ground Floor were all lined in marble and bronze artwork would be used to decorate these spaces.

The centrepiece of the First Class lounge was an 18th century Adams-style fireplace and waiting passengers would sit in neo-Georgian green upholstered settees and armchairs making use of occasional tables and writing desks with shaded electric lamps scattered about on a rose-pink carpet. The walls were in distemper and there was a silence telephone cabinet. Cunard publicity would claim the lounge "an apartment which, if it has an equal, has certainly no superior among public rooms in public offices".

This Ground Floor space was previously occupied by the Pacific Steam Navigation Company

Natural light was provided by great windows whose arched crowns rose to 15 feet above the sills to the beautiful coffered ceiling. Electric lamps were suspended from the ceiling, the clusters being concealed in open saucer-like shells, whose opalescence ensured thorough diffusion of the light which added to the subdued effect.

Second and Third Class were dealt with on the Lower Ground Floor in the Basement along with the stores, safes and luggage. Both classes had a waiting area, cafes, Baggage Department, Stores, Shipping and Customs' Department, and Despatch and Stationery Departments.

Second Class passengers experienced a "comfort is everywhere" approach and their department took up the north west corner and had a special entrance from Water Street, together with a separate entrance to the Main Office on the Ground Floor. Comfortably upholstered settees were provided and a number of small tables and chairs where passengers would find writing materials, magazines and timetables to occupy their time.

The large cafe adjacent would act as a supplementary waiting room with toilet accommodation. The entire department was well-lit with windows opening on the west and north sides and there was a lift to access all floors, including the roof restaurant.

Third Class facilities were found on the Lower Ground Floor on the north side of Water Street and were specially designed to meet the "peculiar and exacting" requirements of this class.

Above is the Second Class Passengers' Cafe and, below, the facilities for Third Class travellers

A view from Cunard Building showing Mauretania at the landing stage

Emigrants from all over Europe had to face the ordeal of a medical examination and forms to complete before embarking. Cunard was anxious to reassure them they would experience in the Building some little foretaste of the "unremitting care and attention that has won Cunard ships a unique reputation with this class of ocean traveller".

Third Class passengers would be dealt with expeditiously after entering this extensive suite of offices by a revolving door and a broad stairway which led into a well-lit central hall with a floor space of 300 yards. On two sides of the hall were counters behind which Cunard officials would collect passage money, change money and issue tickets, rail orders and inspection cards.

Passengers would receive their berthing numbers so when they embarked their ship it would be into cabins already allocated to them. Hundreds of passengers could not be dealt with within minutes so those who had to wait could do so comfortably in the ventilated central hall while adjacent was a large buffet where tea, coffee and light refreshments were served and a cloak room.

According to Cunard: "In short, the general spaciousness of the Cunard Building has enabled the Company to make such complete arrangements concerning the handling of their Third Class traffic as will appeal to passengers quite as much as the steps taken to ensure their safety and comfort on ship board."

"I have no doubt that you can only feel the 'soul' of the city when you stand at Pier Head with the Three Graces behind you"

John Flamson, left, spent eeight years working in Cunard Building for Government Office North West. Right, former Deputy Prime Minister John Prescott

THE END OF THE CORRIDOR

The scale and nature of the business conducted by Cunard in its Liverpool Headquarters had huge ramifications for both the city, especially its port, and the country as a whole.

More than 30 years after Cunard left for Southampton, the Building would once again become home to people making momentous decisions for the city – decisions which on many occasions also influenced the government of the day.

In 1994, Government Offices were set up in England's regions. Government Office Merseyside (GOM) was initially based inside a bleak, Sixties office block at Graeme House, close to the Victoria Monument in Derby Square. It later became Government Office North West.

"The move from Graeme House to the prestigious Cunard Building was a statement of confidence in the city, enhancing not diminishing the Government's presence in Liverpool," says John Flamson, the former Deputy Regional Director of Government Office North West. He spent eight years in the organisation working at Cunard Building and has many memories of the working environment and the actions taken there which shaped the city Liverpool is today.

The period when GONW occupied its Cunard Building space was one of enormous and significant milestones in Liverpool's regeneration. Much of what we see today was made possible by major funding and other issues discussed and agreed on the Ground Floor.

John Flamson directed the Objective 1 Programme 2000-2008.

"It had a partnership governance structure. It made for some rumbustious meetings in the Building, but overall the mood was positive. Cunard Building saw many people from all the sectors pass through its doors."

Big grants went to the Merseyside Special Investment Fund to stimulate investment in new and existing businesses in Merseyside.

"John Prescott as Deputy Prime Minister and a former Cunard employee was of course smitten by the Building." he says. "So were other Government Secretaries of State and Ministers. I recall a visitor entering our open plan area heading to my office saying that he felt he was coming into something that was a cross between the Bank of England and the British Library. Playfully, I suggested to him that that was exactly the impression that we liked to give – a blend of authority and erudition!"

Most departments of Government were represented within GONW in Cunard Building, with the exception of the Treasury and Cabinet Office.

"It meant that people in Merseyside had access to Government on their doorstep," he says. "I have no doubt that you can only feel the 'soul' of the city, indeed you can only feel the point of the city, when you stand at Pier Head with the Three Graces behind you and look out to sea.

"I was in front of the Graces in the late 1980s showing a visiting Australian architect around. We were looking out towards New Brighton when suddenly we were joined by an 'old salt', who had obviously been on the rum since sunrise.

"He put his arm around the shoulder of our Aussie friend, who true to type didn't flinch. Our interloper pointed down river then in the thickest Scouse accent I had ever heard said: 'Turn right for America. Turn left for Africa. Straight on for Ireland, you can't miss it!' And with that he meandered off towards the city centre between those twin pillars of maritime history: Cunard Building and the Port of Liverpool Building. In his inimitable way he had captured the city's inextricable and inextinguishable link with the sea. The Mersey is more than a river – it is a gateway and a threshold, and Cunard Building is one of its sentinels."

As the new European Director, he again found inspiration from the Building.

"I was asked to address a full-team meeting. Many of them were career civil servants and were probably wondering who this new guy was, as he hadn't been promoted from within the ranks.

"The Mersey is more than a river – it is a gateway and a threshold, and Cunard Building is one of its sentinels"

"I reminded them that they were Government and need not be browbeaten by anyone. I pointed out that we were housed in a Building that was once a symbol of commercial power, a Building that represented confidence in the city's future. So, I wanted them to believe that they also had public power and could change not just the landscape of Merseyside but its business competiveness, its skills levels and its image – they could change people's lives. I don't think I could have made such a speech in a pokey, low ceilinged, utilitarian office shell."

Cunard Building left a notable impression.

"I loved its exterior design and its situation," says Mr Flamson. "But inside, I always enjoyed attending or chairing meetings in the stylish ground floor meeting room on the river side of the central reception corridor. Here you could see out of the windows and instantly be part of the city's identity. It helped keep one's thinking in perspective, notwithstanding the enormity of some of the challenges we faced. A former colleague of mine summed up what I often felt in that room: 'History teaches us that we have the capacity to change things.'

"Colleagues in London used to refer descriptively to GONW inside the Cunard Building as 'the end of a very long corridor'. This was important for GONW's authority. It was not beholden to a higher authority. It was part of that higher authority."

No 1 Liverpool

In June 1969, Cunard Building was put up for sale for £3 million but Cunard was keen to stress this did not mean it was actually leaving the property as the intention was to lease back the 80,000 square feet occupied by its cargo shipping interests. It was also announced the Building was producing a gross income of £183,000 a year.

According to Cunard: "The idea behind the arrangement is simple. By selling the Building, Cunard passes the responsibility for its upkeep over to the people who make property their business. More importantly, the transaction will release a substantial capital sum for Cunard to plough back into its real business – shipping."

At this time the Building was included in the Ministry of Housing and Local Government's list of buildings of special architectural and historic interest. Tenants included ICI, Spillers, HM Customs, Canada Life, the Consulates-General of the USA and France and the Booth Steam Ship Co. Cunard Building was sold to Prudential plc for £2,750,000 in December 1969 in what was then the biggest Liverpool property sale involving a single building.

Cunard would maintain a presence there until October 1978 when, after 61 years, it moved to Cunard House in the city's Cotton Exchange Building on Old Hall Street. The move was "in the interest of overall efficiency" and included the operations of the General Agency for Atlantic Container Line, H E Moss & Co. Ltd, shipbrokers, Radio & Electronic Services, accounts, office services and fleet medical and welfare services.

Cunard's Three Queens – Queen Mary 2, Queen Victoria and Queen Elizabeth – together on the River Mersey as part of the line's 175th anniversary celebrations

Cunard had been planning a major overall of its space in the Cunard Building – the first since selling it almost 10 years earlier – when the Cotton Exchange Building became available and it made sense to relocate to a more modern building in the heart of Liverpool's commercial centre. Moving into new accommodation already fitted out avoided a period of months when rebuilding and refurbishing would cause disruption, inconvenience and discomfort to the 160 staff being relocated.

Cunard would maintain a presence in the city until the early 1990s through its cargo operations, which by then were located in Mercury Court, but the sale of Cunard Ellerman at this time ended any physical connection the Company had with the city. However, regular visits by Cunard ships maintained the line's association with its 'spiritual home'.

One key project that had agonised senior management in Cunard Building in the 1960s was the replacement for Queen Mary and Queen Elizabeth, and the eventual decision was to build the truly revolutionary and epoch-making Queen Elizabeth 2. And after that decision was taken, following nerve-wracking false starts and near disasters, the Building became – along with the shipyard itself – the powerhouse of design and decision-making that led to Cunard's most successful ship ever.

QE2 would salute Cunard Building during eight visits to the Mersey but the first visit, on Tuesday 24 July 1990, as part of Cunard's 150th anniversary celebrations, was perhaps the most memorable as a million people lined the banks of the Mersey to see her spectacular maiden arrival. All subsequent visiting Cunarders would pay tribute to the Building as it stood as a physical reminder of where Cunard had come from.

Over the years, various rumours about the potential use of Cunard Building as a hotel would surface and several schemes would be rumoured and then be quietly forgotten. On 14 September 2001, the Building was sold for £17,700,000 to Wirral Metropolitan Borough Council which was acting for the Merseyside Superannuation Pension Fund, an organisation that provided pension services to 100,000 public sectors workers in Liverpool. Tenants at this time

The Cotton Exchange Building on Old Hall Street and, right, Cunard Building being cleaned up and a meeting of dock workers at the Pier Head in 1972

included a variety of public and private sector organisations including Government Office North West.

The new owners embarked on a £4 million refurbishment of the Building in 2002 in order to attract new tenants to a key property on a potential World Heritage Site. Accommodation was made available on the Lower Ground, Third, Fourth, Fifth and Sixth Floors in various sizes from 500 square feet to more than 8,000 square feet. One suite on the Fourth Floor overlooked the Strand and covered more than 8,000 square feet, this being made possible by the removal of a maze of offices.

Because of the historic significance of the Building, attention was given to ensuring that decor and fittings remained but the architects were careful to use clever designs so that the new suites met modern requirements such as installing raised flooring for easy IT installations.

The Pier Head, including the Three Graces, as well as several other areas in the city, were indeed declared a World Heritage Site by UNESCO in 2004 – gaining international recognition as being of special cultural or physical significance.

In November 2008, it was announced Cunard Building managers had appointed local architects firm Buttress Fuller Alsop Williams to draw up a conservation plan, involving English Heritage and the Local Authority Conservation Officer, to preserve the Building. The plan would be used to control any future modification and repairs.

Further work on the Building would commence in June 2010 and included the common public areas, the cleaning of the exterior shell and stone repairs. At times over the decades the Portland stone had appeared blackened by pollution, and cleaning would take two years and cost around £2.5 million.

The extensive refurbishment also involved restoring all of the ornate ceilings and fluted columns as well as the mahogany panelled doors and brass ironmongery throughout the Building, including the giant central staircase. Interestingly, the refurbishment of the lift cars resulted in marble from the same Italian quarry as the original marble being obtained.

Conference and dining facilities were made available for tenants and the wider business community and the Sixth Floor offered a 12-

THREE QUEENS, ONE MAGNIFICENT CITY – AND A PALACE!

Some 47 years after Cunard moved its UK headquarters out of the Building bearing its name, the famous Pier Head edifice once again became the focal point of international interest in the passenger shipping line.

On 16 April 2014, first details of Cunard's 175th anniversary salute to its 'spiritual home' were revealed during a special presentation made in the former Public Office Hall on the Ground Floor.

Mayor of Liverpool Joe Anderson welcomed Cunard Director Angus Struthers to speak to an invited audience representing dozens of organisations from Liverpool who would all have a major part to play in the greatest maritime event ever witnessed on the Mersey. The rendezvous of Queen Mary 2, Queen Victoria and Queen Elizabeth may have been set to take place immediately outside the Building, but it was what was said inside that day that made headlines around the world.

In the year that followed the announcement, and before the fleet gathered at Liverpool, the Building continued to play a major part as the finishing touches were put to a plan five years in the making.

During leave ashore, Cunard Commodore Christopher Rynd, Captains Kevin Oprey and Chris Wells together with Cunard's Marine and Nautical Manager Andrew Hall attended "3QL" planning meetings in former Board Rooms at Cunard Building.

Elsewhere inside, work went on to facilitate the huge media interest the 175 events were already attracting. Locations to launch giant fireworks from the roof were also identified and tested, and the complex arrangements required to turn the riverside facades of all Three Graces into giant screens for a stunning light and laser projection show during the Three Queens weekend were finely tuned at Cunard Building.

Throughout the days and evenings of 24-26 May when the Cunard fleet saluted its spiritual home, the Building played host to

Angus Struthers, left, and Joe Anderson with a painting depicting a fictional meeting on the Mersey between the Cunard's first ship Britannia and today's flagship Queen Mary 2

operational meetings to keep the event running smoothly as well as VIP receptions hosted by the City Council and other tenants.

More than 1.3 million spectators descended on the banks of the Mersey to witness the greatest event of its kind ever staged – an event made possible by Three Queens, One Magnificent City – and a Palace! Five weeks later, the Building again took centre stage as the 175th Anniversary of the paddle-steamer Britannia departing Liverpool for the first time, bound for North America, was celebrated by the return to the Mersey of Queen Mary 2 to embark on a special recreation of the 1840 voyage.

The Building had been at the centre of the celebrations with images and TV footage beamed around the world. How proud those who created Cunard Building more than a century ago would be!

And how bemused they might have been had they glanced from their office windows on a bright winter's day in 2016 to see the Lord Mayor of Liverpool, Cllr Tony Concepcion, together with Cunard's Angus Struthers driving a flock of sheep across the Pier Head in celebration of Cunard's admission to the City of Liverpool's Freedom Roll of Association, the highest civic honour Liverpool can bestow and granted on board Queen Mary 2 at Liverpool during the 2015 celebrations.

seat Board Room, the 50-seat Queen Mary Suite, the 60-seat Cunard Suite and the 110-seat Banquet Suite.

At this time the Building was being marketed appropriately as: "The Cunard. No Ordinary Building".

No ordinary building indeed and one that was to become no ordinary base for Liverpool City Council as in October 2013 the authority approved its acquisition for use as offices and cruise liner terminal for £10.3 million.

A further £5 million would be spent on relocating 1,000 council staff from Millennium House and leases in the Capital Building, saving an estimated £1.3 million.

The initial plan to house a cruise terminal in the grand spaces on the Ground Floor was subsequently dropped thanks to insurmountable logistical issues and astronomical costs but the Council has announced plans for the Ground Floor spaces including the opening of the British Musical Experience and around £6 million being spent being spent on two restaurants, including one 500-seat dining space.

By the end of 2015, an independent valuation of the Building concluded it was worth £27.8 million with a potential to bring in an additional £2 million per year in rents. This underlined its value and significance, and came at the end of a year when the Building had played a central role in Cunard's 175th anniversary celebrations in its 'spiritual home'

And into 2016, a year when Cunard Building celebrates its 100th anniversary as the third and final Grace joins her sisters in the '100 Club'. The Port of Liverpool Building reached the milestone in 2007 while the Liver Building followed suit in 2011.

The anniversary will be formally celebrated on Saturday 2 July when Queen Elizabeth arrives on the Mersey to salute this magnificent Building.

Other events, including concerts on the Pier Head, a Civic Reception and Dinner on board Queen Elizabeth and fireworks, will pay tribute to the Passenger's Palace but anything taking place pales into insignificance when compared to the importance of, and contribution made by, Cunard Building over the last 100 years.

Mayor of Liverpool Joe Anderson with the keys to Cunard Building following its purchase by the city council